The Quc

Krishnamurti

The Quotable
Krishnamurti

Compiled by
Robert Epstein

QUEST
BOOKS

Theosophical Publishing House
Wheaton, Illinois • Chennai, India

Compilation copyright © 2011 by Robert Epstein
First Quest Edition 2011

> Quest Books
> Theosophical Publishing House
> P. O. Box 270
> Wheaton, IL 60187-0270
> www.questbooks.net

Cover photo: Indian spiritual teacher
Jiddu Krishnamurti (1895–1986),
courtesy The Mary Evans Picture Library.

The publisher wishes to thank the Krishnamurti Foundation in
America for permission to quote from *Commentaries on Living:
First*, *Second*, and *Third Series*.

Library of Congress Cataloging-in-Publication Data

Krishnamurti, J. (Jiddu), 1895–1986.
The quotable Krishnamurti / edited by Robert Epstein.—1st Quest ed.
    p.   cm.
Includes bibliographical references.
ISBN 978-0-8356-0890-9
1. Conduct of life—Miscellanea. 2. Life—Miscellanea. I. Epstein,
Robert.
II. Title.
B5134.K751 2011
181'.4—dc22   2010053375

Printed in the United States of America

5   4   3   2   1   *   11   12   13   14   15

Lovingly dedicated to my nieces
Alyson Adler
and
Rebecca Epstein

CONTENTS

ACKNOWLEDGMENTS

The editor would like to thank the following people for their love and support during the course of this project: Louise and Mel Adler, Evelyn Epstein, Martin Epstein and Suzanne Kalten, Sophie Soltani, Jay Schlesinger, Wendy Etsuko Siu, and Miriam Wald. Special thanks to Nancy Oken, who one afternoon at work shared a quote from Krishnamurti, which inspired the idea for this book.

I am also very grateful to Richard M. Smoley and Sharron Dorr at Quest Books, who enthusiastically endorsed the book idea from the beginning, and to the Krishnamurti Foundation of America for granting permission to use quotations from Krishnamurti's published works.

Finally, I wish to express deep appreciation to my longtime partner, Stacy Taylor, whose interest in Krishnamurti and editorial skill have been instrumental at all stages of this project.

> *Love is: dying every day. Love is not memory; love is not thought. Love is not a thing that continues as duration in time. And, through observation, one must die to the continuity of everything. Then there is love; and with love there comes creation.*
>
> –J. Krishnamurti,
> quoted in Ravi Ravindra,
> *Two Birds on One Tree*

A Brief Note
on the Text

Please note that all italics appear in the original. Brackets [ ] represent clarifying content supplied by the editor. British spelling has been modified for an American readership, and minor changes in punctuation and spelling have been made in the interest of clarity and modernization. The editor has chosen to leave the exclusive reference to the male gender intact, as Krishnamurti wrote at a time when female pronouns were not commonly alternated with male pronouns to represent humanity and as to insert them in the text would be cumbersome for the flow of reading. Finally, the editor takes full responsibility for any errors in the representation of Krishnamurti's words found in the text.

The source of each quotation appears in parentheses immediately following the quote. The author's name is given only when the author is someone other than Krishnamurti. For full publishing information, see the bibliography.

The majority of quotations in this book come from the three-volume series by Krishnamurti called *Commentaries on Living*. While the volumes were originally published by the Krishnamurti Foundation, the ones used for page citations here were republished by Quest Books in 1967 and reprinted as follows: first series, twelfth printing, 2006; second series, ninth printing, 2002; third series, tenth printing, 2007. Shortened citations are used for quotes from this series. For instance, (2, 216) means the quote appears on page 216 of the second series of the *Commentaries*, Quest Books' ninth printing, 2002.

INTRODUCTION

———————

Once every thousand years or so, an individual appears who turns the world on its head, who questions everything that is taken to be sacrosanct. Jiddu Krishnamurti was such a man.

Krishnamurti was born into a Brahmin family on May 11, 1895, in the small town of Madanapalle, some distance from Madras in the ancient culture of India, the birthplace of another revolutionary teacher, Siddhartha Gautama. As a boy, Krishnamurti was wide-eyed and dreamy, seemingly lost in a world of his own. He and his younger brother, Nityananda, were an inseparable pair. They were spotted by Charles W. Leadbeater, a clairvoyant leader of the Theosophical Society, as the boys were ambling on the beach of the Theosophical Society's Indian headquarters, where their father had come to live and work following the death of Krishnamurti's beloved mother in 1905.[1] Leadbeater beheld an extraordinary aura surrounding Krishnamurti and divined that the starry-eyed boy would become the vehicle of Lord Maitreya to make his appearance as the World Teacher. Curiously, Leadbeater's intuition echoed both what Krishnamurti's mother had felt prior to Jiddu's birth and the thoughts of an astrologer whom she had consulted about her eighth baby's horoscope.

In the midst of a spiritual whirlwind, the teenaged Krishnamurti, together with Nitya, was separated from his father for strict training, education, and purification, which lasted well into his twenties. Surrounded by wealth and elegance, Krishnamurti emerged a highly disciplined, if deferential and cultivated, young man of British manners who had been initiated into the occult world of the Theosophists.[2] A special organization called the Order of the Star grew up around him, as he was heralded far and wide as the World Teacher, an avatar.

Anticipation was intense, and thousands were in attendance on August 2, 1929, the day that Krishnamurti was to formally assume the helm of the Order. What he did was utterly unprecedented and contrary to all self-interest. Krishnamurti summarily dissolved the Order of the Star and admonished its devotees to pursue their own individual freedom without recourse to any doctrine, tradition, or religious organization. His stirring words, first declared on that day in 1929 when he was thirty-four years old, ring no less true today:

> *Truth is a pathless land, and you cannot approach it by any path whatsoever; by any religion, by any sect. . . . My only concern is to set men absolutely, unconditionally free.*[3]

From that day on, with a hiatus only during World War II, Krishnamurti traveled the globe for more than sixty years, giving talks in one city after another, year after year, with unwavering passion, intensity, clarity, and conviction. What was it that K, as he referred to himself, wanted with all his heart for people to see, to realize, to act upon?

Frequently, as he began his talks before audiences large or small, Krishnamurti would implore listeners to attend wholeheartedly, suspending the impulse to agree or argue, to aver or condemn. Krishnamurti reminded those in attendance that he had no wish to be revered or regarded as a sage, spiritual authority, guru, or holy man. Rather, he sought to engage simply in dialogue as though between friends—a dialogue characterized first and foremost by genuine interest, mutual respect, and reciprocal affection. This earnest request on Krishnamurti's part was in no way pretentious or peripheral to the teaching he offered to the thousands who sought his wisdom and insight. On the contrary, they were natural manifestations of his teachings, at the heart of which was *love*.

No attempt is made here to restate the core of Krishnamurti's wisdom. In addition to being presumptuous, such an undertaking—within the scope of a brief introduction—would be deeply disrespectful to Krishnamurti, who spent a lifetime refining his understanding of what it meant to live fully. In fact, Krishnamurti found it necessary himself to remind others tempted to assume the mantle of spokesperson: "From the nineteen twenties I have been saying there should be no interpreters of the teachings."[4]

Hence, the rationale for presenting Krishnamurti in his own words. Still, as Krishnamurti himself observed time and again, "The word is not the thing." Words can deceive, words can hypnotize, words can obscure fact or truth. Above all else, Krishnamurti admonished both readers and listeners to set aside their habitual inclinations to filter words and ideas through an evaluative mill, judging them on the basis of past knowledge or experience. Krishnamurti had come to understand that nothing new could be realized, no radical change could occur, if the conditioned mind was relied upon as the primary means for encountering what is new and unfamiliar.

For Krishnamurti, the habit-driven mind, which human beings everywhere have inherited over thousands of years of evolution, is so constituted for the purpose of survival. The organism's primitive instinct for survival embeds fear in consciousness, so we are nearly always on guard, poised to fight or flee. Krishnamurti understood that the instinct for physical survival infiltrated the psychological realm—a terrible turn, in his estimation—as it solidified an ego or center, called the self, that overrelies upon thought, prior knowledge, and memory at the expense of freedom, truth, and creative action.

Krishnamurti stressed again and again that he was not anti-intellectual (opposed to progress in

science, technology, medicine). He clearly understood, and appreciated, that thoughts, theories,
and knowledge have their place; what he ques-
tioned—and he was unique in doing so—is their
penetration into the psychological realm, resulting
in confusion, fragmentation, inaction.

For Krishnamurti, human dependence on
thought as it manifests in religions, nation states,
and cultural and ethnic identities has resulted in
conflict, animosity, exploitation, and war since
time immemorial. While public policy wonks,
economic pundits, and pious religious leaders have
argued sanctimoniously about the superiority of
their cherished beliefs, the world has been burning.
Often Krishnamurti would declare to audiences:
"The house is on fire," yet they stared back quizzi-
cally, expectantly, lulled by a lifetime of conditioning into waiting passively for the guru or savior to
guide them to safety.

Krishnamurti steadfastly refused to play the
messiah. He insisted that each person be a light

unto him- or herself. Through meditative awareness, which he distinguished from the so-called
methods and techniques of hypnosis masquerad-
ing as meditation, one could find one's own way
to freedom, love, and action. Krishnamurti had an
unwavering conviction in an innate intelligence
that had nothing to do with intellect—that part
of the brain cultivated by conventional education,
which is little more than the civilian equivalent of
military conformity and obedience.

What Krishnamurti called for was nothing less
than revolution, but not the so-called revolution that
the American colonists or the French, the Russians,
or the Cubans had fomented, which he regarded as
puerile. Instead, he envisioned an inward revolution
based on love that would divorce the individual from
allegiance to the State, the Church, and all other affil-
iations and organizations.

Love is the only true revolution, Krishnamurti
taught. But he was not urging a New Age form of
love, induced by psychedelics or diluted cultural

relativism, but a fierce love that was inseparable from what Krishnamurti referred to as *the Inexhaustible* or *the Immeasurable*. For Krishnamurti, love rendered all measurement, judgment, and comparison completely null and void. Love transcends time; love transcends knowledge, image, memory, and ideal. Love is the only true source of action and renewal; it is also what brings about intimacy with death, because from the vantage point of love, life and death are inextricably connected, not separate.

In short, love restores the awareness that one is and has always been whole, undivided. Love enables me to see that I am more than a skin-encapsulated ego: I am, by my very nature, related to everyone and everything, including the animals, ocean, coral, and trees. In the absence of love, we live lives of quiet desperation, inwardly isolated, enfeebled by the hope of gradual self-improvement or redemption in the hereafter.

Reincarnation and the afterlife are illusions clung to by a frightened self in search of permanence, Krishnamurti ardently maintained. He had little patience with the persistent questions he received about heaven and eternity. Such queries took one away from, rather than brought one closer to, that which is beyond the field of the known.

There was one thing, and one thing only, that Krishnamurti was interested in: what *is*.[5] All else was a distraction, as far as Krishnamurti was concerned. To apprehend what *is,* all fear has to end, not by force or will, but by dint of alert observation. If one realizes that everything one has thought, believed, and done has wrought havoc in one's life, this all-encompassing realization brings one to a full stop. One doesn't need to try a second time to determine if a lit stove will burn one's hand again; once learned, the learning lasts an entire lifetime. This learning is the instantaneous fruit of what Krishnamurti termed *choiceless awareness.* Choiceless awareness *is* loving intelligence. Loving intelligence is not external to us, to be found in cathedrals or temples or mosques. Loving intelligence is right here, right now ... beyond the limits of time in which the conditioned self lives. Right thinking, skillful action in one's everyday life, flows naturally when loving intelligence is unobstructed by slavish attachment to the crutches we rely on for security: identification with parties, deities, ideologies, and above all, ideals.[6]

"God is disorder," Krishnamurti once remarked during a talk. He shocked many in the audience. It was a shock designed to jolt one out of the consensus trance we typically inhabit until we reach our graves.

In your hands is a collection of insights and truths, originating in love and compassion, to jolt you into full attention. Krishnamurti was awake; will you dare to join him in wakefulness and make your own revolution? "You are the world," Krishnamurti avowed; in our own hands lie the weapons of destruction . . . or the plowshares of peace.

Robert Epstein
December 21, 2009
El Cerrito, California

NOTES

1. According to biographer Mary Lutyens, Krishnamurti was devastated by his mother's death when he was ten, but, as his mother had been clairvoyant, he saw her on more than one occasion after she was cremated. Krishnamurti recalled: "My mother's death in 1905 deprived my brothers and myself of the one who loved and cared for us most. . . . In connection with my mother's death, I may mention that I frequently saw her after she died" (Mary Lutyens, *Krishnamurti: The Years of Awakening,* 5). It is unclear how his mother died, but it may have been due to malaria, which was prevalent in the area at the time.

2. In 1922, Krishnamurti underwent an excruciatingly painful initiation, which continued over an extended period of time, whereby his body, mind, and soul were prepared for the great spiritual work as World Teacher for which he was being groomed. For an account of "the process," as Krishnamurti called it, see Lutyens, *Krishnamurti: The Years of Awakening.*

3. Lutyens, *Krishnamurti*, 293, 297.

4. Ibid., 233.

5. What *is* includes controversy surrounding Krishnamurti's intimate life, although this is beyond the scope of

the present book. A decades-long love relationship that Krishnamurti had with Rosalind Ragapogal is recounted in her daughter Radha Rajagopal Sloss's book, *Lives in the Shadow with J. Krishnamurti*. While some have blindly defended Krishnamurti, accusing the author of perpetrating vicious rumors, others have summarily dismissed Krishnamurti's teachings based on the belief that he was a hypocrite. The fact is that Krishnanmurti never held himself up to be a role model or saint free of human needs. Ravi Ravindra, an associate of Krishnamurti who raised questions about the congruence between his message and his personality or behavior, suggested that Krishnamurti, like other great teachers, was beset by a "sacred schizophrenia." Such sensationalistic terminology is not only grossly inaccurate—having a private affair is not a criterion of psychosis, nor is intentional dishonesty—but a major affront to the depth of understanding and wisdom that Krishnamurti embodied. Were he alive, it is not hard to imagine Krishnamurti inviting one and all to engage in an exploration of one's reactions, whatever they happened to be, in the spirit of self-understanding.

6. Krishnamurti may have been the only one among his contemporaries to critique Gandhi's ideal of nonviolence. For him, striving to achieve such an ideal was the very antithesis of a truly religious life, which is

centered on facing what *is*. During a public talk in 1981, Krishnamurti observed: "Non-violence is an absurd idea, an invention, an escape. It does not exist" (*Krishnamurti at Rajghat*, p. 103). Unflinchingly facing the truth of one's own violence was, for Krishnamurti, the beginning of wisdom, order, and transformation.

~ Acceptance ~

Acceptance implies that there is an entity who accepts, does it not? And is not this acceptance also a form of effort in order to gain, to experience further?

(2, 216)

~ Acquisitiveness ~

The mind is not quiet when it is acquiring or becoming. All acquisition is conflict. (2, 38)

Every acquisition is a form of boredom, weariness. We want a change of toys; as soon as we lose interest in one, we turn to another. (2, 24)

Does not acquisition dull the mind? Acquisition, positive or negative, is a burden. As soon as you acquire, you lose interest. (2, 25)

~ ACTION ~

Action is always in the present, and is therefore immediate. (1, 48)

Any action which is not comprehensive, total, must inevitably lead to sorrow. There is only total human action, not political action, religious action, or Indian action. (3, 60)

Action based on authority is no action at all; it is mere imitation, repetition. (3, 218)

Unified or integrated action cannot take place as long as there's conflict between opposing parts of the mind. (3, 216)

~ ALONENESS ~

It is strange how we are never alone, never strictly
alone. We are always with something, with a problem,
with a book, with a person; and when we are alone,
our thoughts are with us.   (2, 44)

To be alone, in the highest sense, is essential.
                                             (2, 10)

Isolation can never give birth to aloneness; the one
has to cease for the other to be. Aloneness is indivisible and loneliness is separation.   (1, 11)

To the alone, life is eternal; to the alone there is
no death.   (1, 11)

One is alone, like the fire, like the flower, but one
is not aware of its purity and of its immensity. One
can truly communicate only when there is aloneness.
                                             (1, 11)

There is an aloneness which is not this loneliness, this sense of isolation. That state of aloneness is not a remembrance or a recognition; it is untouched by the mind, by the word, by society, by tradition. It is a benediction. (3, 272)

~ AMBITION ~

Why are we clever and ambitious? Is not ambition an urge to avoid what *is*? . . . Why are we so frightened of what *is*? What is the good of running away if whatever we are is always there? (1, 245)

Where there is ambition, there is no love; and action without love has no meaning. (3, 21)

Ambition breeds mediocrity, for ambition is the fulfillment of the self through action, through the group, through idea. (2, 285)

~ Anger ~

Anger cannot be got rid of by the action of will, for will is part of violence. (1, 74)

To be free from violence, which is not the cultivation of nonviolence, there must be the understanding of desire. (1, 74)

~ Animals ~

In the West we think that animals exist for the sake of our stomachs, or for the pleasure of killing, or for their fur. In the East it has been taught for centuries and repeated by every parent: do not kill, be pitiful, be compassionate. (2, 236)

Killing for so-called sport, for food, for one's country, for peace—there is not much different in all this. Justification is not the answer. There is only: do not kill. (2, 236)

If your motive is not that of really helping the animals, then you are using them as a means to your self-aggrandizement, which is what the bullock-cart driver is doing. (3, 35)

~ ARROGANCE ~

Surely, to know, to be certain, is the way of vanity, arrogance. As long as one knows . . . there is only continuity; and what has continuity can never be in that state of creation which is the timeless. (3, 135)

~ THE ASCETIC ~

Our living is always partial, never whole, and thereby we make ourselves insensitive. Through suppression of desire, through mere control of the mind, through denial of his bodily needs, the ascetic makes himself insensitive. (3, 395)

Is it necessary to lead a hermit's life in order to abnegate the self? You see, we have a concept of the selfless life, and it is this concept which prevents the understanding of a life in which the self is not.   (2, 242)

~ ATTACHMENT ~

Conditioning is attachment: attachment to work, to tradition, to property, to people, to ideas, and so on. If there were no attachment, would there be conditioning? Of course not.   (2, 5–6)

To cultivate detachment is another form of escape, of isolation; it is attachment to an abstraction, to an ideal called detachment.   (2, 7)

Attachment has no nobility. . . . Attachment is self-absorption, whether at the lowest or at the highest level.   (1, 123)

Attachment implies fear, does it not? . . . As long as you are occupied with the pleasure of attachment, fear is hidden, locked away, but unfortunately it is always there. (2, 267–68)

~ ATTENTION ~

Attention frees the mind from habit. (3, 29)

To start with facts, and not with assumptions, we need close attention; and every form of thinking not originating from the actual is a distraction.

(3, 197)

Do we ever listen to anything with attention, or do our thoughts, our interpretations, and so on, interfere with our listening? (3, 200)

Surely, attention has no motive, no object, no toy, no struggle, no verbalization. This is true attention, is it not? Where there is attention, reality *is*. (3, 200)

When the mind is on the flight of discovery, imagination is a dangerous thing. . . . Speculation and imagination are the enemies of attention. (3, 257)

If you want to understand, you will have to give your attention, and there's no attention when one part of your mind is concerned with results, and the other with understanding. In this way you get neither.

(3, 287)

What fluctuates is not attention. Only inattention fluctuates. (Ravindra, *Two Birds*, 69)

~ AUSTERITY ~

Austerity is the simplicity of inward aloneness, the simplicity of a mind that is purged of all conflict, that is not caught in the fire of desire, even the desire for the highest. Without this austerity, there can be no love, and beauty is of love. (3, 31)

~ AUTHORITY ~

The worship of authority, whether in big or little things, is evil, the more so in religious matters.

(1, 67)

Authority engenders power, and power always becomes centralized and therefore utterly corrupting.

(1, 102)

You accept authority, as the guru also does, in order to be safe, to be certain, in order to be comforted, to succeed, to reach the other shore. (3, 21)

Authority corrupts, whether in high places or among the thoughtless. The thoughtless are not made thoughtful by following another, however great or noble he may be. (2, 211)

No authority knows; and he who knows cannot tell.

(3, 288)

The very questioning of authority is the end of
authority.   (3, 21)

~ AWARENESS ~

Thought cannot come to an end save through passive
watchfulness of every thought. In this awareness there
is no watcher and no censor; without the censor, there
is only experiencing.   (2, 32)

Awareness, without any choice, of the ways of the
mind, which is the breeder of illusion, is the beginning of meditation.   (1, 89)

The mind can be aware of its own bondage, and in
that very awareness it is learning.   (3, 330)

Being aware of the truth and the falseness of seeking, the mind is no longer caught in the machinery of
seeking.   (3, 295)

B

~ BALANCE ~

Balance is nonacquisitiveness.   (1, 44)

~ BEAUTY ~

If beauty is merely an opposite, it is not beauty.
                                            (3, 413)

Meditation is the way of life, it is part of daily existence, and the fullness and beauty of life can only be understood through meditation.   (3, 194)

It was a beautiful evening. The sky was flaming red behind the rice fields, and the tall, slender palms were swaying in the breeze.   (1, 274)

Beyond the woods was the lovely, curving river. . . .
The water was deep and cool, and always flowing. It
was a beautiful thing to watch, so alive and rich.

(3, 39)

She was carrying a large basket on her head, holding
it in place with one hand; it must have been quite
heavy, but the swing of her walk was not altered by
the weight. She was beautifully poised, her walk easy
and rhythmical. (3, 43)

In a small house, a woman with a clear voice was sing-
ing; it brought tears to your eyes, not from nostal-
gic remembrance, but from the sheer beauty of the
sound. You sat under a tree, and the earth and the
heavens entered your being. (3, 192)

Pick up a piece of shell. Can you look at it, wonder at its
delicate beauty, without saying how pretty it is, or what
animal made it? . . . If you can, then you will discover
an extraordinary thing, a movement beyond the
measure of time, a spring that knows no summer.

(3, 265)

Over the palm trees could be seen a great stretch of pale blue sky, which the clouds were rushing to cover. Among the people, along the noisy streets, and in the gardens of the well-to-do, there was great beauty; it was there everlastingly, but few cared to look.

(3, 325)

~ BECOMING ~

Becoming is the continuation of time, of sorrow. Becoming does not contain being. (1, 4)

Becoming and being are two widely different states, and you cannot go from one to the other; but with the ending of becoming, the other is. (2, 174)

~ BEING ~

There is no being if there is a struggle to be. (1, 30)

Being is always in the present, and being is the highest form of transformation.   (1, 4)

~ BELIEFS ~

Belief, religious or political, sets man against man. So-called religions have divided people, and still do. Organized belief, which is called religion, is, like any other ideology, a thing of the mind and therefore separative.   (2, 19)

The other name for belief is faith, and faith is also the refuge of desire.   (1, 56)

Belief conditions experience, and experience then strengthens belief. What you believe, you experience.
                                  (1, 94)

One of the curses of ideologies and organized beliefs is the comfort, the deadly gratification they offer. They put us to sleep.   (1, 195)

~ BLISS ~

There is great bliss in meditation.   (2, 260)

Search is born of conflict, and with the cessation of conflict there is no need to seek. Then there is bliss.
(3, 25)

~ BONDAGE ~

Suppression and conformity are not the steps that lead to freedom. The first step toward freedom is the understanding of bondage.   (2, 280)

Freedom *from* something is not freedom; it's only a reaction, the opposite of bondage. Freedom is when bondage is understood.   (3, 296)

Meditation is the breaking of all bondage; it is a state of freedom, but not *from* anything.   (2, 197)

[Self-]realization is possible only when the mind is no longer in bondage to time. (3, 383)

∾ BOREDOM ∾

Interest, curiosity, is the beginning of acquisition, which soon becomes boredom; and the urge to be free from boredom is another form of possession. (2, 26)

∾ THE BRAIN ∾

Compassion can never exist where the brain is conditioned or has an anchorage.

(Ravindra, *Two Birds*, xvii)

The brain can function effectively, naturally, and easily, only when there is harmony, noncontradiction, and complete stability, that is, only when there is real order. (*Krishnamurti at Rajghat*, 81)

~ BUDDHA ~

The Buddha comes closer to the basic truths and facts of life than any other. . . . Although I am not myself a Buddhist, of course.

(Weeraperuma, *Living and Dying,* 108)

To the Buddhist, the word *Buddha*, the impression, the image, creates great reverence, great feeling, devotion; he seeks refuge in the image which thought has created. And as the thought is limited, because all knowledge is always limited, that very image brings about conflict. (*Total Freedom*, 145)

~ CAUSE AND EFFECT ~

There is no freedom within the network of cause [and] effect. (3, 296)

All cause [and] effect is within the sphere of self-centered activity. (3, 386)

Is there a state without cause? Is not love such a state? (3, 419)

~ CERTAINTY ~

This very desire to be certain, to be secure, is the beginning of bondage. (3, 196)

~ Change ~

Can there be change through an act of will? Is not will concentrated desire? . . . Desire cannot bring about fundamental change. . . . As long as the mind, or desire, seeks to change itself from *this* to *that*, all change is superficial and trivial. (2, 232)

Change within the pattern [of society] is no change at all; it is mere modification, reformation. Only by breaking away from the social pattern without building another can you "help" society. (3, 110)

Haven't you noticed that when you say, "I will try to change," you have no intention of changing at all? You either change, or you don't; *trying* to change has actually very little significance. (3, 216)

Be simple with the fact that you don't want to change. The realization of this truth is in itself sufficient.
(3, 217)

~ CHASTITY ~

Chastity is not a thing of the mind; chastity is the
very nature of love. (2, 68)

~ CHOICELESS AWARENESS ~

What is important, surely, is to be aware without
choice, because choice brings about conflict. The
chooser is in confusion, therefore he chooses; if he is
not in confusion, there is no choice.

(First and Last Freedom, 97)

~ CITY LIFE ~

Life in a city is strangely cut off from the universe;
man-made buildings have taken the place of valleys
and mountains, and the roar of traffic has been substituted for that of the boisterous streams. (1, 121)

As with all cities, there was an atmosphere of depression and unnameable sorrow in contrast to the light of the evening. . . . We seem to have forgotten what it is to be natural, to smile freely; our faces are so closed with worry and anxiety.   (1, 126–27)

The streets were like canyons between the tall buildings, and there were no trees. It was noisy; there was the strange restlessness of a people who had everything and yet nothing.   (2, 225)

~ CIVILIZATION ~

Civilizations may vary according to climate, environment, food, and so on, but culture throughout the world is fundamentally the same: to be compassionate, to shun evil, to be generous, not to be envious, to forgive, and so on. Without this fundamental culture, any civilization, whether here or there, will disintegrate or be destroyed.   (2, 220)

~ CLARITY ~

Clarity cannot be given by another.   (1, 68)

~ COMMUNION ~

Relationship implies communion with another on different levels; and is there communion with another when he is only a tool, a means of my happiness?

(1, 108)

~ COMPARISON ~

There are so many ways of escaping from ourselves, and comparison is one of them.   (1, 45)

When you compare yourself with others, it is to justify or condemn what you do, and then you are not thinking at all.   (3, 36)

Comparison does not bring about understanding; comparison is another form of distraction, as judgment is evasion. (2, 149)

~ COMPASSION ~

The compassionate man knows right action.
(3, 228)

Compassion is not hard to come by when the heart is not filled with the cunning things of the mind.
(2, 264)

~ CONCENTRATION ~

Concentration implies a dual process, a choice, an effort, does it not? There is the maker of effort and the end toward which effort is made. So concentration strengthens the "I," the self, the ego as the maker of effort, the conqueror, the virtuous one. (2, 281)

Concentration is the way of desire.   (2, 280)

Concentration in meditation is a form of self-centered improvement; it emphasizes action within the boundaries of the self, the ego, the "me."   (2, 279–80)

~ CONCLUSIONS ~

Setting out with a conclusion, or looking for a preconceived answer, puts an end to right thinking; in fact, there is then no thinking at all.   (3, 207)

We always want to get a result in return for doing something. This desire for a result, which is another form of conclusion-seeking, prevents understanding.
(3, 287)

To think from a conclusion is not to think at all. It's because the mind starts from a conclusion, from a belief, from experience, from knowledge, that it gets caught in routine, in the net of habit.   (3, 361)

~ CONDITIONING ~

There is no noble or better conditioning; all conditioning is pain.   (3, 43)

~ CONFLICT ~

Conflict exists only in exploitation and not in relationship.   (2, 37)

The understanding of conflict is the understanding of desire.   (1, 61)

~ CONFUSION ~

When one is confused one seeks guidance, but that which one finds will invariably be the outcome of one's own confusion.   (2, 210)

~ Consciousness ~

The whole movement of consciousness is the response
of the past.   (3, 400)

Consciousness as the experiencer, the observer, the
chooser, the censor, the will, must come to an end,
voluntarily and happily, without any hope of reward.
The seeker ceases. This is meditation.   (2, 198)

The urge to interpret must cease before there can be
the understanding of the whole process of consciousness.   (2, 251)

Most of us are aware of only a small corner of it [the
totality of consciousness], and our lives are spent in
that small corner, making a lot of noise in pushing
and destroying each other, with a little friendliness
and affection thrown in.   (3, 320–21)

Can there be an ending of consciousness as continuity, a dying to the total feeling of becoming without
gathering again in the very act of dying?   (3, 343)

~ Consistency ~

To be consistent is to be thoughtless.   (1, 115)

The desire to be consistent gives a peculiar strength and satisfaction, for in sincerity there is [the illusion of] security.   (1, 115)

How we admire a man who is consistent, who sticks to his conclusion, to his ideal! Such a man we consider a saint. But the insane are also consistent; they also stick to their conclusions.   (1, 141)

~ Contentment ~

Contentment is never the outcome of fulfillment, of achievement, or of the possession of things; it is not born of action or inaction. It comes with the fullness of what *is*, not in the alteration of it.   (2, 271)

Contentment, perhaps, is an ugly word, but real contentment does not imply stagnation, reconciliation, appeasement, insensitivity. Contentment is the understanding of what *is*, and what *is* is never static.

(1, 250)

Contentment is a state of nondependency. . . . There must be freedom to be content.

(2, 54)

Contentment is the complete understanding of what *is* from moment to moment.

(2, 130)

Contentment is above and beyond the opposites; it is not a synthesis, for it has no relation to conflict. . . . Contentment is a movement that is not of time.

(2, 130)

~ CONTROL ~

Control is evasion. You may control a child or a problem, but you have not thereby understood either.

(1, 239)

~ CONVERSION ~

Conversion is change from one belief or dogma to
another, from one ceremony to a more gratifying one,
and it does not open the door to reality.　　　(1, 18)

~ COOPERATION ~

To work together through fear or through greed for
reward is not cooperation. Cooperation comes naturally and easily when we love what we are doing; and
then cooperation is a delight.　　　(3, 33)

Cooperation is possible only when there is freedom
from envy, acquisitiveness, and from the craving for
personal or collective dominance, power.　　(2, 211)

~ COURAGE ~

The calm mind means also courage, so that you may
face without fear the trials and difficulties of the Path.

(At the Feet, 53)

~ CRAVING ~

There is no entity separate from craving; there is only
craving, there is no one who craves.   (1, 113)

Craving is remembrance; there is no craving without
the known, which is the memory of what has been,
and it is this craving that sustains the "me," the self,
the ego.   (3, 343)

The craving to *be*, negatively or positively, is the
denial of virtue of the heart.   (1, 30)

The craving to experience must wholly cease, which
happens only when the experiencer is not nourishing
himself on experiences and their memories.   (1, 69)

~ CRUELTY ~

The ways of cruelty are many and subtle.   (3, 226)

Without love, you cannot comprehend cruelty; a peace of sorts may be established through the reign of terror, but war, killing, will continue at another level of our existence.   (3, 229)

If you see a case of cruelty to a child or an animal, it is your duty to interfere.   (*At the Feet*, 49)

~ CURIOSITY ~

Mere curiosity does not lead very far.   (3, 401)

Curiosity is not the way of understanding. Understanding comes with self-knowledge. He who suffers is not curious; and mere curiosity, with its speculative overtones, is a hindrance to self-knowledge.   (1, 8)

~ DEATH ~

It is simple to die, and it is hard to continue; for continuity is effort to be or not to be. Effort is desire, and desire can die only when the mind ceases to acquire.
(2, 23)

Death is the new, and life as continuance is only memory, an empty thing. With the new, life and death are one.
(1, 247)

We are frightened of ending; but without ending, how can there be the new? Without death, how can there be life?
(1, 246–47)

We separate life from death, and so both remain unknown.
(3, 102)

Death is the unknown. The problem is not what death is and what happens thereafter, but for the mind to cleanse itself of the past, of the known. Then the living mind can enter the abode of death, it can meet death, the unknown. (2, 256)

Whatever we may know about it, death itself cannot be brought into the field of the known. (2, 71)

~ DEATH ANXIETY ~

Fear comes in the movement away from the fact [of death], the what *is*. Belief [in an afterlife], however comforting, has in it the seed of fear. (2, 255)

Life and death are inseparable, and in their separation lies everlasting fear. Separation is the beginning of time; the fear of an end gives birth to the pain of a beginning. (2, 240)

~ Dependency ~

Dependence breeds possessiveness, envy, fear; and then fear and the overcoming of it become your anxious problem. (1, 108)

Dependence grows stronger, escape more essential, in proportion to the fear of what *is*. (1, 225)

~ Desire ~

Desire does not bring contradictions. Desire *is* contradiction. (3, 354)

If you destroy desire, you destroy sensitivity, as well as the intensity that is essential for the understanding of truth. (3, 396)

The desire to be is the beginning of complexity. (1,32)

It is a fact that all desire is one and the same, and we cannot alter that fact, twist it to suit our convenience and pleasure, or use it as an instrument to free ourselves from the conflicts of desire; but if we see it to be true, then it has the power to set the mind free from breeding illusion. (2, 142)

Desire is never satisfied; there is no end to desire. (2, 244)

∼ DISCIPLINE ∼

Discipline is the suppression, the overcoming of what is. [As such, it] is a form of violence. . . . [But] through resistance, how can there be the free, the true? (2, 30)

Discipline is a process of condemnation, comparison, or justification. (2, 31)

Discipline implies compulsion, subtle or brutal, outward or self-imposed; and where there is compulsion, there is fear. (2, 30)

~ DISCONTENT ~

Discontentment is a flame that must be kept burning brightly. . . . Discontent is painful only when it is resisted. (3, 101)

Contentment and discontent are like the two sides of one coin. To be free from the ache of discontent, the mind must cease to seek contentment. (3, 102)

We are discontented because we think we should be contented; the idea that we should be at peace with ourselves makes discontentment painful. (3, 360)

To be integrated with discontent . . . is to allow that which has no opposite, no second, to come into being. (2, 179)

Discontent is part of existence, but . . . [o]ne way or another, most of us manage to smother this flame of discontent, don't we? . . . [I]s it possible to keep it always burning? And is it then discontent?   (3, 360)

~ DISCOVERY ~

If there were guidance, there would be no discovery. There must be freedom to discover, not guidance. Discovery is not a reward.   (2, 246)

~ DREAMS ~

The dream is not real. The dream is often taken for the real, but the dream and dreamer are the occupation of the mind.   (1, 188)

Dreaming is the continuation of the conscious state, the extension of which is not active during the waking hours.   (1, 187))

If you can be . . . aware, constantly watching, listening, you will find that you do not dream at all. . . . To such a mind, dreams are unnecessary.   (3, 323)

~ DYING TO THE KNOWN ~

Dying to the known is the complete stillness of the mind.   (3, 343)

How necessary it is to die each day, to die each minute to everything, to the many yesterdays and to the moment that has just gone by! Without death there is no renewing; without death there is no creation.   (2, 8)

The mind is always afraid of coming to an end. But, living is ending from day to day; it is the dying to all acquisition, to memories, to experiences, to the past.
                                                             (2, 26–27)

Only that which has an ending can be aware of the new, of love, or the supreme. . . . The mind must die to the past, though the mind is put together by the past. (3, 344)

Die [psychologically] to the whole of our existence not little by little, but totally! . . . You must die to all of the known for the unknown to be. (3, 143)

~ EARTH ~

How extraordinarily beautiful and rich the earth is!
There is no tiring of it. (2, 270)

This earth is ours; it is not the earth of the Brahmin,
the Russian, or the American. We torture ourselves
with these inane divisions. (3, 154)

~ EDUCATION ~

Integrated life and action is education. . . . To help
[the child] understand the ways of authority and not
be caught in the net of society is education. (3, 61)

In education there is neither the teacher nor the taught, there is only learning; the educator is learning, as the student is. (3, 62)

To educate a student to conform to society is only to encourage in him the deteriorating urge to be secure. (3, 93–94)

To be rightly educated is not just to have studied history or physics; it is also to be sensitive to the things of the earth—to the animals, to the trees, to the streams, to the sky, and to other people. (3, 161)

Without goodness and love, you are not rightly educated. (3, 152)

If you want to be rightly educated, you have to set about it yourself. . . . Education is the cultivation of the mind so that action is not self-centered. (3, 151)

~ EFFORT ~

Effort to be or not to be something is the continuance of the self. (3, 132)

Effort, conflict, cannot under any circumstances bring understanding, and so it is a degenerating factor in the individual as well as in society. (2, 60)

Effort is desire. . . . Desire breeds deception, illusion, contradiction, and the [illusory] visions of hope.
(2, 197)

~ EMPTINESS ~

Emptiness holds the miracle of life. (1, 21)

Let your heart be wholly empty; then only will it be filled. (1, 169)

When the heart is empty of the things of the mind, and the mind is empty of thought, then is there love. That which is empty is inexhaustible. (1, 185)

~ Evil ~

There is no enlightened following; all following is evil. (2, 211)

Evil cannot become good, for that which is good is not the product of thought; it lies beyond thought, like beauty. (*Total Freedom*, 162)

Three sins there are which work more harm than all else in the world—gossip, cruelty, and superstition—because they are sins against love. (*At the Feet*, 66)

In everyone and in everything there is evil. . . . We can strengthen [it] by thinking of it, and in this way we can help or hinder evolution; we can do the will of Logos or we can resist it. (*At the Feet*, 67)

~ EXPERIENCE ~

The desire for the repetition of an experience, whether your own or that of another, leads to insensitivity, to death. (1, 64)

Experience can never bring freedom from sorrow; experience is not an adequate response to the challenge of life. (1, 99)

~ EXPERIENCING ~

In the state of experiencing, there is neither the experiencer nor the experienced. . . . The experiencer must cease to experience, and only then is there being.
(1, 28)

The state of direct experiencing is attention without motive. (3, 253)

With most of us, experiencing is always becoming memory. (2, 156)

Experiencing, in which there is neither the experiencer nor the experienced, is beyond conflict.

(1, 194)

~ Experimentation ~

To experiment is not to seek a definite result. If you seek a definite result, experiment is not possible.

(1, 268)

~ Exploitation ~

To exploit is to be exploited. The desire to use others for your psychological necessities makes for dependence ... and what you possess, possesses you. (1, 101)

~ FACTS ~

A fact in itself has no opposite; it has an opposite only when there is a pleasurable or defensive attitude.

(1, 48)

The gathering of facts does not make for the understanding of life. (3, 4)

Truth is not a matter of conviction or agreement. You can agree or disagree about opinions or conclusions, but a fact needs no agreement; it's so. (3, 168)

It is foolish to be angry with a fact. Avoidance of a fact through anger is one of the commonest and most thoughtless reactions. (1, 285)

~ Falseness ~

If you want to know the truth or the falseness of the
fact, then you must not live in the word, in the intellect.
(3, 288)

What is false must be put away if what is true is to be.
(3, 389)

To see the false as the false is in itself enough, for
that very perception frees the mind from the false.
(2, 283)

~ Family ~

As long as the family is a center of security, there will
be social disintegration; as long as the family is used
as a means to a self-protective end, there must be
conflict and misery. (2, 133)

The family as it is now is a unit of limited relationship, self-enclosing and exclusive. . . . The family as a means of inward security is a source of disorder and social catastrophe. (2, 132)

~ FEAR ~

Fear is not to be put away by appeasements and candles; it ends with the cessation of the desire to become. (1, 68)

Fear is uncertainty in search of security. (1, 164)

It is the desire not to see [things as they are] that brings on fear; and when you don't want to understand the full significance of what *is*, fear acts as a preventive. (2, 74)

Fear exists in the conflict of the opposites. The worship of success brings the fear of failure. (1, 164)

~ FEARLESSNESS ~

Fearlessness is not courage but freedom from accumulation.
(2, 39)

~ FOLLOWING ~

To look for light from another, without self-knowledge, is to follow blindly. All following is blind.
(3, 66)

Following is merely a symptom of a deep longing for security.
(3, 66)

He who follows another, whether it be the greatest saint or the teacher round the corner, is essentially irreligious.
(3, 311)

Following another, whether it be a leader, a savior, or a Master, does not bring about clarity and happiness.
(2, 210)

~ Forgiveness ~

Forgiveness is unnecessary when there is no accumulation of anger. (1, 73)

Forgiveness is essential if there is resentment; but to be free from flattery and from the sense of injury, without the hardness of indifference, makes for mercy, charity. (1, 73–74)

~ Freedom ~

Freedom is the only means to freedom. (2, 36)

Freedom is and must always be at the beginning; it is not an end, a goal to be achieved. One can never be free in the future. (2, 54)

~ FULFILLMENT ~

There is the ceaseless pursuit of fulfillment, in whose very shadow is frustration; so we never know or experience wholeness of being.   (3, 395)

Fulfillment is the way of covering up inward poverty, emptiness, and in fulfillment there is sorrow and pain.   (1, 92)

Self-fulfillment is a vain pursuit, isn't it? In the very fulfillment of the self, there is fear and disappointment.   (3, 102)

Not to gather, but to die each day, each minute, is timeless being. As long as there is the urge to fulfill, with its conflicts, there will always be the fear of death.   (2, 189)

The search for permanency is the everlasting cry of self-fulfillment.   (1, 92)

~ THE FUTURE ~

Are not wars, the increasing disasters and misery, the outcome of our daily life? . . . The future is in the present; the future will not be very different if there is no comprehension of the present.   (1, 243)

As long as the mind thinks in terms of changing through time, of bringing about a revolution in the future, there is no transformation in the present.
(3, 126)

What is the future of mankind, the future of all those children you see shouting, playing—such happy, gentle, nice faces—what is their future? The future is what we are now. . . . You see on television endless entertainment from morning until late in the night. . . . The children are entertained. The commercials all sustain the feeling that you are being entertained. And this is happening all over the world. What will be the future of these children?
(*Total Freedom*, 139–140)

~ GENEROSITY ~

To be generous with the hand is one thing, but to be generous of heart is another. (1, 23)

~ GOD ~

The fear of uncertainty, of not being, makes for attachment, for possession. . . . The ultimate gratifying possession is the word *God*, or its substitute, the State. (1, 181)

The thought of God is not God, it is merely the response of memory. (1, 190)

To find truth, or God, there must be neither belief nor disbelief. . . . To seek God without understanding oneself has very little meaning. (3, 181)

Surely, to know love, truth, God, there must be no opinions, no beliefs, [and] no speculations with regard to it. (3, 288)

We can find out the truth or the falseness of God only when the word *God* no longer creates in us certain habitual physiological or psychological responses.
(3, 227)

If you know you are experiencing God, then that God is the projection of your hopes and illusions.
(2, 136)

~ GOSSIP ~

How oddly similar are gossip and worry. They are both the outcome of a restless mind. (1, 6)

To talk about another, pleasantly or viciously, is an escape from oneself, and escape is the cause of restlessness. Escape in its very nature is restless. (1, 6)

~ GRATIFICATION ~

To seek lasting gratification at any level of our being is to bring about confusion and sorrow; for gratification can never be permanent. (1, 86)

~ GREED ~

The desire to conserve energy [in the search for truth] is greed. This essential energy cannot be conserved or accumulated; it comes into being with the cessation of contradiction within oneself. (3, 396)

To be greedy... you must strive, compete.... [Without] this drive, you are not free of greed but only self-enclosed. (1, 23)

~ HABIT ~

The cultivation of habit, however good and respectable, only makes the mind dull. (3, 27)

The mind forms habits in order to be secure, safe, certain, undisturbed, in order to have continuity. . . . The mind moves . . . from one certainty to another; so there's never freedom from the known. (3, 383)

Habit is mechanical, and to resist it is only to feed the machine, give more power to it. (3, 383)

The more one struggles against a habit, however deep its roots, the more force one gives to it. To be aware of one habit without choosing and cultivating another is the ending of habit. (2, 232)

To be inwardly alert, to think anew about your work, about the absurdities of society, to find out for yourself the true significance of religion—it is this that will free the mind from being enslaved by any habit.

(3, 28)

∼ HAPPINESS ∼

Happiness *through* something must invariably beget conflict, for then the means is vastly more significant and important than happiness itself. (1, 108)

Happiness is not an end in itself. It comes with the understanding of what *is*. Only when the mind is free from its own projections can there be happiness.

(2, 85)

When one is happy, time is nonexistent, yesterday and tomorrow are wholly absent; one has no thought for the past or the future. (2, 111)

~ HELP ~

When you do not seek it, help comes. It may come from a leaf, from a smile, from the gesture of a child, or from any book. But if you make the book, the leaf, the image, all-important, then you are lost, for you are caught in the prison of your own making.

(3, 245)

If someone has helped you and you make of him your authority, then are you not preventing all further help, not only from him but from everything about you? (2, 228)

There is help everywhere for a man who is alert; but many of us are asleep to everything about us except to a particular teacher or book, and that is our problem.

(2, 226–227)

When you are open, there is unending help in all things, from the song of a bird to the call of a human being, from the blade of grass to the immensity of the heavens. (2, 228)

~ HOPE ~

To live happily is to live without hope. The man of hope is not a happy man, he knows despair. (2, 112)

The mind, with its incessant weaving of patterns, is the maker of time; and with time there is fear, hope, and death. Hope leads to death. (2, 115)

Hope and despair are words that cripple the mind with their emotional content, with their seemingly opposing and contradictory urges. (2, 263)

Disciplines [such as meditation, yoga, fasting] cannot offer freedom; they may promise, but hope is not freedom. (2, 122)

~ HOW ~

The [question of] "how" is a new way to acquire.
(2, 157)

The important thing is to keep awake, and not ask *how* to keep awake; the pursuit of the "how" is the urge to be safe. (2, 238)

The "how" is the process of inquiry, it is not the search for a method. If one is seeking a method, then inquiry has stopped. (3, 252)

There is no "how." There is only understanding, the impulse that will shatter the old. (3, 306)

~ HUMANITY ~

To help all, you must understand all.
(*At the Feet*, 57)

The earth is ours, it is not English, Russian, or American, nor does it belong to any ideological group. We are human beings, not Hindus, Buddhists, Christians, or Muslims. All these divisions have to go, including the latest, the Communist, if we are to bring about a totally different economic-social structure.   (3, 60)

~ HUMILITY ~

To follow is to deny humility. . . . The pursuit of an ideal prevents humility, for the ideal is the glorification of the self, the ego.   (2, 147)

Wisdom and truth come to a man who truly says, "I am ignorant, I do not know." The simple, the innocent, not those who are burdened with knowledge, will see the light, for they are humble.   (2, 149)

There's no inquiry if there's no humility. To learn, there must be humility.   (3, 371)

To practice humility is to cultivate pride.   (3, 372)

~ "I" ~

So the "I" is put together by the feeling or desire which arises through the natural response of seeing [an appealing object]. Without seeing, sensing, desiring, is there an "I" as a separate, isolated entity?

(3, 300)

~ IDEALS ~

Ideals can never bring about a fundamental revolution, but only a modified continuity of the old.

(1, 142)

The myth, the ideal, is unreal; it is a self-projected escape, it has no actuality.

(1, 139)

Thought projects the ideal; the ideal is part of thought. The ideal is not something beyond thought; it is thought itself. (1, 197)

The pursuit of the ideal is the search for reward. . . . The ideal is a compensation, a fictitious state which the mind has conjured up. (2, 99)

~ IDEAS ~

To approach what *is* with an idea, a conclusion, a dream, is not to understand what *is*. Prejudiced observation is no observation at all. (2, 21)

Fear exists only in relationship to an idea, and idea is the response of memory as thought. (1, 113)

It is not our problems which set man against man, but our ideas about them. Problems bring us together, but ideas separate us. (1, 244)

Idea and belief are the very antithesis of love. (2, 83)

~ IDENTIFICATION ~

Identification is vicarious experience, and hence utterly false. (1, 5)

Love is vulnerable, pliable, receptive; it is the highest form of sensitivity, and identification makes for insensitivity. Identification and love do not go together, for the one destroys the other. (1, 5)

Identification with the great is still a projection of the small. . . . The small in search of the large will find only what it is capable of finding. (2, 48)

~ IGNORANCE ~

Ignorance is one thing, and the state of not knowing is quite another; the two are in no way connected. You may be very learned, clever, efficient, talented, and yet be ignorant. (3, 236)

Ignorance is the lack of self-awareness; and knowledge is ignorance when there is no understanding of the ways of the self. Understanding of the self is freedom from knowledge. (1, 21)

Ignorance is the very process of becoming. (1, 263)

Ignorance of the ways of the self leads to illusion.
(1, 86)

∼ ILLUSION ∽

Illusion is very gratifying, and hence our attachment to it. Illusion may bring pain, but this very pain exposes our incompleteness and drives us to be wholly identified with the illusion. (1, 87)

Is God to be found in churches, or in our hearts? The urge to be comforted breeds illusion; it is this urge which creates churches, temples, and mosques.
(2, 225)

~ IMAGINATION ~

The speculative mind, with its intricate thoughts, is not capable of fundamental transformation; it is not a revolutionary mind. . . . Imagination prevents the perception of what *is*, as does comparison.   (2, 180)

~ IMPERMANENCE ~

There is only one fact: impermanence.   (3, 340)

The search for permanency is the everlasting cry of self-fulfillment; but the self can never fulfill, the self is impermanent, and that in which it fulfills must also be impermanent.   (1, 92)

~ INDIVIDUALS ~

It is only as individuals that we can do anything at all. It has always been an individual, here and there, who has really affected society and brought about great changes in thought and action. (3, 163)

~ THE INEXHAUSTIBLE ~

Wisdom is essential for the coming into being of the unknown, the inexhaustible. (1, 46)

The inexhaustible is not to be discovered through any activity of the mind. (2, 9)

The new is the inexhaustible. (1, 250)

To give, there must be the inexhaustible. (1, 184)

~ INHERITANCE ~

Parents and society are shaping the minds of the children through tradition, belief, dogma, conclusion, opinion, and this psychological inheritance prevents the coming into being of a new social order.   (3, 63)

When you realize very deeply that inheriting property is as destructive as psychological inheritance, then you will set about helping your children to be free from both forms of inheritance.   (3, 63–64)

~ INNOCENCE ~

How simple it is to be innocent! Without innocence, it is impossible to be happy. . . . Innocence is freedom from the burden of experience.   (2, 38)

Knowledge, the burden of the past, is corruption. The power to accumulate, the effort to become, destroys innocence; and without innocence, how can there be wisdom?   (2, 39)

Without dying to the past, how can there be the renewing of innocence?   (1, 237)

~ INTEGRATION ~

Integration, like peace, is a by-product, not an end in itself.   (1, 117)

Integration is a state of complete attention.   (2, 61)

The integrated entity is not made whole by another; because he is complete, there is completeness in all his relationships. What is incomplete cannot be made complete in relationship.   (2, 110–111)

~ INTELLIGENCE ~

Intelligence is not a cumulative result, but freedom from progressive achievement and success.   (1, 49)

Simplicity is the way of intelligence—not the mere show of simplicity in outward things and behavior, but the simplicity of inward nonbeing.   (3, 236)

When you say "I know," you are on the path of nonintelligence; but when you say "I don't know," and really mean it, you have already started on the path of intelligence. (3, 236)

Intelligence is to be discovered in freedom. (1, 49)

Intelligence is a matter of hard work, quick perception of the subtle tricks of the mind, facing the fact, and clear thinking, without assumptions or conclusions. To kindle the fire of intelligence, and to keep it alive, demands alertness and great simplicity. (3, 235)

Negative thinking is the highest form of intelligence. (2, 84)

~ INTERPRETATION ~

A mind that is interpreting, translating what *is*, is caught in its own prejudice of satisfaction. Interpretation is not understanding. (1, 250)

~ JEALOUSY AND ENVY ~

Envy is encouraged and respected, is it not? The competitive spirit is nourished from childhood.

(2, 265)

Where jealousy is, obviously love is not; and yet with most people, jealousy is taken as an indication of love.   (1, 9)

Ownership breeds hatred. We really hate what we possess, which is shown in jealousy.   (1, 157)

Success is pursued in different ways, success as an artist, as a business man, as a religious aspirant. All this is a form of envy, but it is only when envy becomes distressing, painful, that one attempts to get

rid of it. As long as it is . . . pleasurable, envy is an
accepted part of one's nature.   (2, 266)

~ JOY ~

Only in discovery can there be joy—the discovery
from moment to moment of the ways of the self.

(1, 70)

All [our] desire for something—for joy, for God, or
whatever it be—is transient. . . . If you realize the
truth of this, then transience itself is joy.   (3, 25)

In dying there is joy.   (2, 8)

Suddenly you heard the clear notes of a flute; and
along the path you met the player, a mere boy. He was
never going to be a professional, but there was joy in
his playing.   (3, 238)

Beyond the bridge is the sea, blue and distant. . . . The city people come here in their cars with their well-dressed children, who shout with the joy of being released from their tight homes and barren streets.

(3, 306)

~ JUSTICE ~

Where there's friendship, compassion, the organization of justice is unnecessary; and through the organization of justice, compassion does not necessarily come into being. On the contrary, it may banish compassion.

(3, 310)

~ KARMA ~

Karma is the reaction which arises from certain causes and produces certain results. . . . Essentially, the process of time is karma, is it not? As long as there is a past, there must be the present and the future.

(2, 94)

Karma is not an ever-enduring chain; it's a chain that can be broken at any time. What was done yesterday can be undone today; there's no permanent continuance of anything.

(3, 377)

Karma is the process of time, the past moving through the present to the future; this chain is the way of thought.

(2, 96)

~ KILLING ~

There are many forms of killing, are there not? There is killing by a word or gesture, killing in fear or anger, killing for a country or an ideology, killing for a set of economic dogmas or religious beliefs.   (3, 223)

With a word or gesture, you may kill a man's reputation; through gossip, defamation, contempt, you may wipe him out. And does not comparison kill? Don't you kill a boy by comparing him with another who is cleverer or more skillful?   (3, 223)

In the paying of taxes, even in the buying of a postage stamp, you are supporting war, the killing of ever-changing enemies.   (3, 224)

~ KINDNESS ~

You don't need philosophies and doctrines to be gentle and kind. . . . Generosity comes from quite a different source, a source beyond all measure.   (2, 264)

How kind we naturally are, especially away from the towns, in the fields and the small villages! (1, 275)

~ KNOWLEDGE ~

Addiction to knowledge is like any other addiction; it offers an escape from the fear of emptiness, of loneliness, of frustration, the fear of being nothing. (1, 21)

The worship of knowledge is a form of idolatry, and it will not dissolve the conflict and misery of our life. ... To know is to deny the unknown. (1, 21–22)

Knowledge is another form of possession. . . . It is much more difficult for the man of knowledge to be free from his possessions than for the man of wealth. (1, 261)

Knowledge is always of the past. (2, 247)

~ LEADERS ~

We choose our leaders, spiritual and political, out of our own confusion, and so they also are confused.
(1, 127)

To have an authority over you, someone to guide you, is very comforting, especially when on all sides there is so much chaos and misery. That is why you become, not exactly a slave, but a follower, carrying out the plan laid down by the leader.
(3, 277)

It doesn't matter what the leaders say, for they are as blind as their followers, otherwise they wouldn't be leaders.
(3, 277)

Recognition is part of the whole process of leadership. Not only does the leader acquire importance, but also the follower.   (3, 312)

Leadership implies power—the power to influence, to guide, to dominate—and, subtly or assertively, these leaders are seekers after power.   (3, 311)

~ LEARNING ~

If we are free to learn, we shall learn from the falling leaf, from every kind of relationship, from being aware of the activities of our own minds.   (3, 330)

Learning is a movement which is not away from or toward something; it ceases when there is the accumulation of knowledge in order to gain, to achieve, to arrive.   (3, 253)

To die to everything that you have learned is to learn.
                                               (3, 332)

A mind that's taught, or desires to be guided, cannot learn.
(3, 331)

The very urgency and importance of being able to learn will free the mind from conclusions, from the self which is put together by words, by memory.
(3, 331)

The self and its maintenance prevent the movement of learning.
(3, 331)

To learn, there must be no accumulation of knowledge, no piling up of experiences as the past.
(3, 330–31)

Being taught has made one repetitive, mediocre. The urge to be guided, with its implications of authority, obedience, fear, lack of love, and so on, can only lead to darkness.
(3, 330)

To a mind that's learning, the heavens are open.
(3, 332)

~ LIFE ~

Life has no beginning and no end; it is both death and life; it is the green leaf, and the withered leaf that is driven by the wind; it is love and its immeasurable beauty; it is the sorrow of solitude and the bliss of aloneness. (2, 149–50)

The understanding of the totality of life brings about its own action, in which there is neither drifting nor the imposition of a pattern. This totality is to be understood from moment to moment. (3, 366)

~ LISTENING ~

Knowledge prevents listening. One may know a great deal; but to listen to something which may be totally different from what one knows, one must put aside one's knowledge. (3, 131)

The very act of listening brings its own freedom. (2, 176)

~ LONELINESS ~

The word "loneliness," with its memories of pain and fear, prevents the experiencing of it afresh.

(1, 113–14)

Love and emptiness cannot abide together; when there is the feeling of loneliness, love is not. (1, 114)

What a strange thing is loneliness, and how frightening it is!

(1, 111)

Loneliness is the awareness of complete isolation.

(1, 112)

We are lonely, but we do not know what it is to be alone. . . . Loneliness, that deep isolation, is the dark shadow of our life.

(2, 102)

Avoiding and overcoming loneliness are equally futile; though suppressed or neglected, the pain, the problem, is still there.

(1, 112)

~ LOVE ~

Love is when there is no fear at any level. (2, 30)

Love is the only true revolution. . . . Only when the flag, the belief, the leader, the idea as planned action, drop away, can there be love; and love is the only creative and constant revolution. (2, 22)

Love that turns to sorrow and to hate is not love.
(1, 266)

To love, the desire for success, for power and position, must cease. One can't have both. (3, 370–71)

Love is never security; love is a state in which there is no desire to be secure; it is a state of vulnerability.
(2, 133)

There is only love, not the love of God and the love of man; it is not to be divided. (3, 26)

~ MEDIOCRITY ~

It is conflict that breeds mediocrity of mind and heart. Freedom from mediocrity is that state which comes into being when all conflict has ceased. (2, 216)

Any desire for self-improvement is petty. When the mind knows that it is mediocre and does not act upon itself, there is the breaking up of mediocrity.

(2, 170)

~ MEDITATION ~

Meditation is freeing the mind of its own thoughts at all levels. (1, 175)

Meditation itself is timeless, it's not a way of arriving at a timeless state. (3, 195)

Meditation is the flowering of goodness; it is not the cultivation of goodness. (3, 368)

The understanding of the activities of the conflicting parts of the mind, which make up the self, the ego, is meditation. (3, 397)

Meditation has nothing to offer; you may not come begging with folded hands. It doesn't save you from any pain. (2, 258)

Meditation is the purgation of the known. (2, 258)

Meditation is a very important action in life; perhaps it is the action that has the greatest and deepest signif-icance. It is a perfume that cannot easily be caught; it is not to be bought through striving and practice.
(2, 258)

If meditation is [done] with intention, the desired
result may be achieved, but then it is not meditation,
it is only the fulfillment of desire.   (2, 243–44)

~ Memory ~

The self is memory, the many conclusions; and
thought is the response of memory.   (1, 178)

Thought can never be free, because all thinking is
the response of memory; without memory, there is
no thinking. Memory, or knowledge, is mechanical;
being rooted in yesterday, it's always of the past.

(3, 314)

~ Mind ~

The problem is the mind itself, and not the problems
it breeds.   (2, 100)

The mind is the result of many thousands of years of tradition and experience. It is capable of fantastic inventions, from the simplest to the most complex. It is capable of extraordinary delusions and of vast perceptions. (2, 281)

You cannot make contradictory desires into a harmonious whole. To attempt to do so is an act of the mind, and the mind itself is only a part. (3, 395)

I am only pointing out that a disciplined, molded mind is not a free mind. With the understanding of desire, discipline loses its significance. (3, 354)

Thought is the product of time, and without the thinking process, time is not. The mind is the maker of time, it *is* time. (2, 127)

Mind is [made up of] time, and thought cannot uncover the measureless. (2, 198)

~ MORALITY ~

Thought creates a division between what *is* and what *should* be, and on this division morality is based; but neither the moral nor the immoral know love. This moral structure, created by the mind to hold social relationships together, is not love but a hardening process like that of cement. (1, 9)

Social morality is mere respectability. Ambition, greed, the conceit of achievement and its recognition, the brutality of power and position, killing in the name of an ideology or a country—this is the morality of society. (3, 175–76)

~ MYTH MAKING ~

Surely one must understand the myth-making mechanism of the mind before there can be the experiencing of that which is beyond the measure of the mind.
(3, 260)

Confusion arises from the conflict between what you are and the myth of what you should be. The myth, the ideal, is unreal; it is a self-projected escape, it has no actuality. The actual is what you are. What you are is much more important than what you should be.
(3, 260)

~ NAMING ~

Conflict ceases when there is no process of naming.
(1, 194)

Without terming or naming, there is no experience.
(1, 194)

Naming has a physiological as well as a psychological effect. When there is no naming, only then is it possible to be fully aware of that which is called the void of loneliness. (2, 270)

~ NATIONALISM ~

Nationalism, like the worship of God, is only the glorification of oneself. (1, 244)

∼ NATURE ∼

And so another day was born. The sun was over the palm trees, and the monkeys were sitting on the wall, their long tails almost touching the earth.　　(1, 152)

It was a lovely morning, pure after the rains. There were tender new leaves on the trees, and the breeze from the sea had set them dancing. . . . How beautiful the earth was, and what a poem of color!　　(1, 205)

Dark clouds were gathering, and the sun was hidden. The earth, the trees, and the whole of Nature seemed to be waiting for another purification.　　(1, 232)

Beyond the yellow sands was the green-gray sea. White waves were crowding onto the beach, but the deep waters were quiet.　　(1, 182)

Below us was a vast sea of clouds, white and dazzling, wave upon wave as far as the eye could see. . . . Occasionally, as we climbed higher in a wide circle, there were breaks in this brilliant foam, and far below was the green earth.　　(1, 222)

How lovely were those red and yellow flowers! Loveliness is not of time. (1, 246)

It was a lovely morning, with clear blue skies, and there was a blessing on the land. The earth was a living thing, bountiful, rich, and sacred. (2, 185)

The view from this hilltop was not breathtaking. . . . You were not a human being, a stranger from a different land, but you were those hills, those goats, and the goatherd. You were the sky and the blossoming earth; you were not apart from it, you were of it. (2, 204)

~ Noise ~

Have you ever tried listening to noise—listening to it as you would listen to music? (3, 412)

If you do not condemn noise, you will find it ceases to disturb the mind. (3, 413)

Noise shuts all things out, it is excluding and isolating; silence includes all things within itself.   (1, 256)

~ NONVIOLENCE ~

Nonviolence is a result, a by-product, and not an end in itself. . . . Nonviolence is not an idea; it cannot be made into a pattern of action.   (1, 121)

The mind thinks in habits; it is conditioned to gradualism, and has come to regard time as a means of achieving freedom from violence. With the understanding of the falseness of that whole process, the truth of violence is seen, and *this* is the liberating factor, not the ideal, or time.   (3, 382–83)

~ NOTHINGNESS ~

It is the fear of being nothing that compels us to accumulate.   (1, 98)

You can come upon your relationship to this nothingness and its fear only by being choicelessly aware
of the escapes.   (1, 98)

You and nothingness are one; you and nothingness
are a joint phenomenon, not two separate processes.
                                                   (1, 98)

~ Now ~

The now has greater significance than the tomorrow.
In the now is all time, and to understand the now is
to be free of time.   (1, 4)

The present being dull, shallow, we turn to the past or
look to a self-projected future. This escape from the
present inevitably leads to illusion. To see the present
as it actually is, without condemnation or justification, is to understand what is, and then there is action
which brings about a transformation.   (1, 133)

~ OPINION ~

Opinion is not truth; we must set aside opinions to find truth. (2, 92)

~ OPPOSITES ~

Is there despair when there is not that state which we call hope? Why should we always think in opposites? . . . If there is to be understanding, is it not necessary to be free of the opposites? (2, 255–56)

Truth is the negation of the false, not the opposite of the false. Truth is entirely different from the positive and the negative, and a mind which thinks in terms of opposites can never be aware of it. (2, 221)

P

~ THE PAST ~

The past is like a shadow, making things dull and weary; in that shadow, the present loses its clarity, its freshness, and tomorrow is the continuation of the shadow.   (1, 186)

How we are bound to the past! But we are not bound to the past: we *are* the past.   (1, 186)

~ PEACE ~

To understand is one thing, and to desire to be at peace is another. With understanding there does come peace, but the mere desire to be at peace only strengthens desire, which is the source of all conflict.   (3, 353–54)

Peace is a state of mind; it is the freedom from all desire to be secure. The mind-heart that seeks security must always be in the shadow of fear.   (2, 221)

Surely, peace comes into being, not through safeguards, sanctions, and guarantees, but it is there when *you* are not—you who are the agent of conflict with your ambitions and frustrations.   (2, 193)

Peace is not with the politician or the priest, neither is it with the lawyer or policeman. Peace is a state of mind when there is love.   (2, 237)

~ PERCEPTION ~

It is easy to perceive what *is*, but to be free of it is another matter; for perception is clouded with judgment, with comparison, with desire. To perceive without the interference of the censor is arduous.

(2, 248)

~ POLITICS ~

Life is not dependent upon political or economic activity; life is not a mere outward show, any more than a tree is the leaf or the branch. (1, 26)

Politics is the reconciliation of effects; and as most of us are concerned with effects, the external has assumed dominant significance. By manipulating effects we hope to bring about order and peace; but, unfortunately, it is not as simple as all that. (1, 26)

~ POSSESSIONS ~

How difficult it is for the man of possessions to be free! It is a great hardship for a rich man to put aside his wealth. (1, 260)

The man who possesses, whether property or knowledge, can never be sensitive, he can never be vulnerable or open. (1, 204)

We possess because in ourselves we are nothing, and in possessing we feel we have become somebody. . . . We are nothing but what we possess—the label, the bank account, the ideology, the person—and this identification breeds enmity and endless strife.

(3, 349)

~ POWER ~

Both poverty and riches are a bondage. . . . Both are corruptible, for both seek that which is corrupting: power.   (1, 81)

The desire for success is the desire for domination.

(1, 82)

To be powerful, to be successful, is to be slavish, which is the denial of virtue.   (1, 81)

Power in any form is evil, and it will inevitably lead to disaster.   (3, 311)

The man who seeks power, or accepts power in any form, is fundamentally irreligious. (3, 313)

What matters is for the mind to free itself from envy, from ambition, from the desire for power, because these destroy compassion. (3, 315)

~ PREOCCUPATION ~

A preoccupied mind is never a free mind, whether it is preoccupied with the sublime or the trivial. (2, 231)

There is a vast difference between a preoccupied mind and an active mind. An active mind is silent, aware, choiceless. (2, 234)

Preoccupation makes the mind trivial, petty, shallow. . . . The mind is petty when it is preoccupied with God, with the State, with virtue, or with its own body. (2, 233)

~ PRETENSE ~

Never pretend to be other than you are, for all pretense
is a hindrance to the pure light of truth.

(At the Feet, 40)

~ PRIDE ~

Hold back your mind from pride, for pride comes
only from ignorance.   *(At the Feet, 55)*

The desire to achieve, to arrive, is part of the pride
which conceals itself in seeking.   (3, 292)

~ PROBLEMS ~

To look for an answer is to avoid the problem—which
is just what most of us want to do. . . . The solution
is not separate from the problem; the answer is *in* the
problem, not away from it.   (1, 106)

No problem is ever old, but we approach it with the old formulations, which prevent our understanding [of] it. (1, 277)

~ Progress ~

How we hug to ourselves the idea of progress. . . . Progress is such a comforting word, so reassuring, a word with which we hypnotize ourselves. (2, 17)

This constant desire for gratification, for more and more subtle forms of sensation, is called progress, but it is ceaseless conflict. (2, 43)

We turn to something in order to acquire; there is acquisition in pleasure, in knowledge, in fame, in power, in efficiency, in having a family. . . . This acquisitive movement is called expansion of thought, progress. (2, 24–25)

~ QUESTIONS ~

It is good to ask questions. You know, we have lost the art of investigation, discussion, not taking sides but looking at things. It is very complex.
(*Total Freedom*, 348)

If you begin to inquire into the question . . . is the answer separate from [it]? Or does the answer lie in the question itself? (*Total Freedom*, 348)

Is that the right question? Irrelevant questions can only produce unimportant answers. (3, 322)

Our only concern is with the question, "Can the mind free itself from its self-created bondage?" (3, 384)

~ REALITY ~

Reality has no continuity; it is from moment to moment, ever new, ever fresh.   (1, 42)

Reality is not of time and is not measurable.   (2, 32)

Reality is not to be reached through detachment; it is unattainable through any means. All means and ends are a form of attachment, and they must cease for the being of reality.   (1, 33)

Reality is not the opposite of illusion. . . . Reality can *be* only when the opposites cease.   (1, 47)

~ REASON ~

If reason is the criterion of action, then the mind can never be free to act. (3, 274–75)

However logical and efficient one's reasoning may be, it does not lead to that which is beyond the mind. For that which is beyond the mind to come into being, the mind must be totally still. (3, 314)

Reason can make one behave in this manner or in that; but what reason has put together, reason can undo. . . . Reason, however subtle and logical, is a process of thinking, and thinking is ever influenced [by] . . . desire or by an idea . . . whether imposed or self-induced. (3, 274–75)

~ REFORM ~

Any reform within the pattern [of society] will, in the end, only cause more confusion and misery. (3, 163)

Mere reforms always need further reform. What is necessary is a total revolution in our thinking.

(3, 247)

~ REINCARNATION ~

The so-called intuition concerning the truth of reincarnation, or life after death, may be merely a wish for survival.

(2, 189)

~ RELATIONSHIP ~

As long as we psychologically need and use each other, there can be no relationship. Relationship is communion; and how can there be communion if there is exploitation?

(2, 37)

There is no end to relationship. There may be the end of a particular relationship; but relationship can never end.

(1, 269)

Only in the mirror of relationship is the mind to be understood, and you have to begin to see yourself in that mirror. (2, 101)

∼ RELATIVISM ∽

The idea that there are separate paths to truth, that truth has different aspects, is unreal; it is the speculative thought of the intolerant trying to be tolerant. (2, 222)

∼ RELIGION ∽

Religion is not a matter of dogmas and beliefs, of rituals and superstitions; nor is it the cultivation of personal salvation, which is a self-centered activity. Religion is the total way of life; it is the understanding of truth, which is not a projection of the mind. (3, 123)

Religion is not a matter of churches, temples, rituals, and beliefs; it's the moment-by-moment discovery of that movement, which may have any name, or no name. (3, 362)

Religion is the feeling of sacredness, of compassion, of love. (3, 315)

A truly religious man is not concerned with politics; to him there is only action, a total religious action, and not the fragmentary activities which are called political and social. (3, 308)

~ RENUNCIATION ~

To give up [as in renunciation] is another form of acquisition. You renounce *this* in order to gain *that*. (1, 180)

Self-sacrifice is an extension of the self. . . . It is still enclosed, petty, limited. (1, 180)

One may see the foolishness of pursuing worldly things
. . . and so one's mind turns to other-worldliness, to the
pursuit of a joy or a bliss which is called God. In the very
process of self-denial is its gratification.   (3, 260)

∼ RESPECTABILITY ∽

Respectability is a curse; it is an "evil" that corrodes
the mind and heart.   (1, 22)

What a strong hold respectability has on us! . . .
Respectability is a cloak for the hypocrite; we commit
every possible crime in thought, but outwardly we are
irreproachable.   (1, 206)

∼ RESPONSIBILITY ∽

Life is a movement not only in time, but also out of time.
[Thus] arises a great responsibility. . . . Responsibility
implies freedom [and] compassion. And the whole of
that is meditation.   (*Krishnamurti at Rajghat,* 84)

~ REVOLUTION ~

Living is the greatest revolution. (2, 118)

Most minds are conservative, they resist change. Even the so-called revolutionary mind is conservative, for once it has gained its revolutionary success, it also resists change. (3, 204)

To be really revolutionary, one must step out of the pattern of society, the pattern of acquisitiveness, envy, and so on. (3, 163)

A limited revolution is no revolution at all. (2, 117)

~ RIGHT THINKING ~

Right thinking is essential for right living. (3, 206)

There's a vast difference, surely, between right think-ing and right thought. Right thinking is constant awareness; right thought, on the other hand, is either conformity to a pattern set by society, or a reaction against society. (3, 206)

Everyday existence, with its ambitions, envies, and so on, must be understood; but to understand it demands awareness, right thinking. There's no right thinking when thought starts out with an assump-tion, a bias. (3, 207)

Setting out with a conclusion, or looking for a precon-ceived answer, puts an end to right thinking; in fact, there is then no thinking at all. So, right thinking is the foundation of righteousness. (3, 207)

~ RITUALS ~

There is a certain amount of beauty and orderliness in ceremonies, but fundamentally they are stimu-lants; and as with all stimulants, they soon dull the mind and heart. (1, 19)

The repetition of chants, of words and phrases, puts the mind to sleep, though it is stimulating enough for the time being. (1, 19)

Rituals are vain repetition which offer a marvelous and respectable escape from self-knowledge. (1, 19)

A mind that is made quiet by discipline, by ritual, by repetition, can never be alert, sensitive, and free. This bludgeoning of the mind, subtly or crudely, is not meditation. (1, 89)

~ ROUTINE ~

We carry on like machines with our tiresome daily routine. How eagerly the mind accepts a pattern of existence, and how tenaciously it clings to it!
(2, 115)

Unless the old pattern [of reliance on knowledge, memory, time] is broken completely there cannot be a radical transformation. (2, 118)

~ SATISFACTION ~

What an ugly thing it is to be satisfied! Contentment is one thing and satisfaction another. Satisfaction makes the mind dull and the heart weary.   (2, 129)

~ SAVAGERY ~

We are obviously savages when we kill thousands for some cause or other, for our country; killing another human being is the height of savagery.   (2, 58–59)

Think of the awful slaughter produced by the superstition that animals should be sacrificed, and by the still more cruel superstition that we need flesh for food.   (*At the Feet*, 72)

~ SECURITY ~

To escape collectively is the highest form of security.
(1, 65)

Surely, only the mind that's not clinging to security is free to discover that which is wholly untouched by the past. (3, 321)

It is this zone of [psychological] safety that most of us are seeking, and it is the desire to be safe, to be secure, that puts us to sleep. (2, 238)

~ SEEKING ~

There is great happiness in not wanting, in not being something, in not going somewhere. . . . The mind is not tranquil as long as it is traveling in order to arrive. (2, 23)

Search arises from the pain of the present, therefore what is sought is already known. (3, 25)

Seeking is a network of activities in which there's no freedom. (3, 295)

Seeking is always measuring, sir. There's no seeking if the mind ceases to measure, compare. (3, 292)

As long as the mind, or desire, seeks to change itself from *this* to *that*, all change is superficial and trivial. (2, 232)

~ THE SELF ~

Every effort of the self to be or not to be is a movement away from what it is. (1, 54)

The activities of the self are frighteningly monotonous. The self is a bore; it is intrinsically enervating, pointless, futile. (1, 107)

The self must end for the new to be. (1, 92)

To be occupied with one's own projections, at whatever level, is to worship the self. (1, 190)

Any activity that gives emphasis to the self, to the ego, is destructive; it brings sorrow. (2, 242)

~ SELF-DISCOVERY ~

Put away the book, the description, the tradition, the authority, and take the journey of self-discovery.
(3, 288)

We are afraid to know ourselves as we are, and this avoidance of what *is* is making us afraid of what *might* be. (2, 74)

~ SELF-HYPNOSIS ~

Without . . . understanding [the self], what is called meditation, however pleasurable or painful, is merely a form of self-hypnosis. (3, 10)

Without understanding the whole complexity of life, and the everyday reactions from moment to moment, meditation becomes a process of self-hypnosis. (3, 194)

~ SENSATIONS ~

Sensations are of the mind, as sexual appetites are.
(1, 110)

Sensations are both pleasant and unpleasant, and the mind holds to the pleasant, thus becoming a slave to them. (1, 110)

Sensation and dissatisfaction are inseparable, for the desire for more binds them together. (1, 271)

~ SENSITIVITY ~

There is good and evil; but to pursue the one and to avoid the other does not lead to that sensitivity which is essential for the being of reality. (1, 47)

How easily we destroy the delicate sensitivity of our being. (1, 55)

Conflict is insensitivity. It is only the sensitive mind that realizes the true. (3, 25)

To be only partly sensitive is to be paralyzed. To be open to beauty and resist ugliness is to have no sensitivity. (3, 185)

~ SILENCE ~

A mind that has been *made* silent is not a silent mind. It's a dead mind. (3, 293)

There can be no silence as long as there is a seeker. (2, 234)

Silence comes with the absence of desire. (2, 92)

Any movement of the mind is a hindrance to silence.
(1, 170)

Silence includes all things within itself. Silence, like love, is indivisible. (1, 256)

Silence is a state totally outside the machinery of the mind. (3, 191)

Noise ends, but silence is penetrating and without end.
(1, 256)

~ SINCERITY ~

The desire to achieve, to gain is the basis of sincerity; and this urge, however superficial or deep, makes for conformity, which is the beginning of fear. (1, 84)

Sincerity can never be simple; sincerity is the breeding ground of the will. (1, 83)

~ SOCIETY ~

Society exists for the individual, and not the other
way round.   (1, 49)

To change society, you must break away from it. You
must cease to be what society is: acquisitive, ambitious, envious, power-seeking, and so on.   (3, 110)

Society is always in a state of degeneration.   (3, 93)

Society, the group, can never be in a state of revolution; only the individual can.   (2, 116)

~ SOLITUDE ~

We are afraid of solitude, for it opens the door to our
insufficiency [and] the poverty of our own being;
but it is solitude that heals the deepening wound of
loneliness.   (2, 103)

~ SORROW ~

Sorrow is sorrow, whether it is yours or mine. . . . The problem of each is essentially the problem of all.

(3, 213)

Sorrow is the result of a shock, it is the temporary shaking up of a mind that has settled down, that has accepted the routine of life. (3, 262–63)

Is sorrow the way of understanding? Or does sorrow exist because there's no understanding? (3, 262)

~ SPACE ~

When the mind has space—which means no direction, no operation of the will and therefore, no fear— there will be silence. (*Krishnamurti at Rajghat*, 84)

Space is necessary, for otherwise you will not be able to see, you will not be able to feel and you will not be free. (*Krishnamurti at Rajghat*, 84)

~ SPONTANEITY ~

Spontaneity is the only key that opens the door to what *is*.   (1, 148)

An occupied mind is not free, spontaneous, and only in spontaneity can there be discovery.   (1, 189)

~ THE STATE ~

The State controls education, it steps in and conditions the human entity for its own purposes; and the easiest way to do this is through fear, through discipline, through punishment and reward.   (2, 58)

Separate nationalities and their sovereign governments, power blocs and conflicting economic structures, as well as the caste system and organized religions—each of these proclaims its way to be the only true way. All these must cease to be, which means that the whole hierarchical, authoritarian attitude toward life must come to an end. (3, 59)

Surely, reform of every kind is also a function of government; it should not be left to the whims and fancies, called ideals, of strong individuals and their groups, for this leads to the fragmentation of the State. (3, 309)

~ State of Search ~

Seeking is the action of the past. But the state of search is entirely different, it's in no way similar to seeking; and it's not a reaction, the opposite of seeking. The two are not related in any way. (3, 294)

Seeking is not the state of search. . . . Seeking, as it's called, is always for something known. Finding is recognizing, and recognition is based on previous knowledge. (3, 294)

~ STILLNESS ~

Do not seek continuity of stillness. Stillness is to be experienced from moment to moment; it cannot be gathered. (2, 252)

~ STIMULANTS ~

Please, I have not taken any drug, because to me any form of stimulant . . . is utterly detrimental, because any stimulant in any form, however subtle, makes the mind dull. (*What Are You Doing?*, 45)

~ SUCCESS ~

Insistence upon success breeds insensitivity, it encourages ruthlessness and self-centered activity. (3, 162)

To succeed is always to fail. Arrival is death and traveling is eternal. (2, 63)

~ SUFFERING ~

To avoid suffering is only to strengthen it.   (1, 200)

~ SUPERSTITION ~

Those who would walk upon the Path must learn to think for themselves, for superstition is one of the greatest evils in the world, one of the fetters from which you must utterly free yourself. (*At the Feet,* 37)

Superstition . . . has caused much terrible cruelty. The person who is a slave to it despises others who are wiser [and] tries to force them to do as he does.
(*At the Feet,* 72)

Many crimes have been committed in the name of the God of love, moved by the nightmare of superstition.
(*At the Feet,* 72)

~ TALENT ~

Talent may become a curse. The self may use and entrench itself in capacities, and then talent becomes the way and the glory of the self. (2, 242–43)

~ THOUGHT ~

Thought cannot penetrate into the unknown, and so it can never discover or experience reality. (1, 42)

The very thinking about what *is* is an escape from what *is*. Thinking about the problem is escape from the problem; for thinking *is* the problem, and the only problem. (2, 7)

Freedom from conditioning comes with the freedom from thinking. When the mind is utterly still, only then is there freedom for the real to be.   (2, 7)

The very process of thinking is the denial of love.

(2, 13)

There is only thought, and thought creates the thinker; thought gives form to the thinker as a permanent, separate entity. . . . But there is only the process of thinking, there is no thinker apart from thought.

(2, 31)

Thought is always a conclusion; thinking is concluding, and therefore it can never be free.   (1, 178)

What we think, we are.   (1, 190)

Thought is the outcome of time; thought is anchored to the past, it can never be free from the past. If thought frees itself from the past, it ceases to be thought.

(2, 257)

Thought is the result of the known, therefore it cannot fathom the unknown, the unknowable.   (2, 223)

The death of thought is life eternal.   (2, 70)

Only when thought ends is there truth.   (1, 191)

~ TIME ~

Seeing that time steals all things, we cling to the time-less.   (1, 32)

Life [experienced] in time is confusion and misery; but when that which *is* is the timeless, there is bliss.   (1, 264)

Time as an abstraction is a mere speculation, and all speculation is vain.   (1, 262)

Surely, there is only chronological time, and all else is deception. There is time to grow and time to die, time to sow and time to reap; but is not psychological time, the process of becoming, utterly false? (1, 262)

Time exists only when there is a psychological gap between what *is* and what *should* be, which is called the ideal, the end. To be aware of the falseness of this whole manner of thinking is to be free from it—which does not demand any effort, any practice.   (3, 11)

We accept certain dogmas and beliefs for various psychological reasons, and through the process of time what is thus accepted becomes "inevitable," a so-called necessity for man.   (2, 172)

~ TOLERANCE ~

Tolerance is of the mind, not of the heart. . . . There is no communion where there is tolerance.   (1, 104)

Tolerance is not compassion, it's a thing put together by the cunning mind. (3, 247)

~ TRADITION ~

The ways of tradition inevitably lead to mediocrity, and a mind caught in tradition cannot perceive what is true. Tradition may be one day old, or it may go back for a thousand years. (3, 4)

~ TRANQUILITY ~

Tranquility does not come into being with abstinence or denial; it comes with the understanding of what *is*. (1, 7)

Tranquility does not begin or end, and a mind thus tranquil is aware of a bliss that is not the reflection of its own desire. (1, 256)

~ TRUTH ~

Truth is the unknown, it cannot be known; if it is known, it is not truth.   (2, 29)

Do you think that you can collect truth as you would money or paintings? Do you think it is another ornament for one's vanity?   (2, 178)

Repetition of a truth is a lie. Truth cannot be repeated, it cannot be propagated or used.   (1, 64)

Truth is not an idea, a conclusion.   (1, 44)

What is true needs no interpretation, and what is interpreted is not true.   (3, 79)

Truth is not to be conquered; you cannot storm it. . . . Truth comes silently, without your knowing.   (2, 67)

Truth is not something to be remembered, stored up, recorded, and then brought out. What is accumulated is not truth.   (2, 79)

~ Ugliness ~

There are people who reject the ugly and cling to the beautiful. . . . But you cannot shut out the ugly and hold to the beautiful without becoming dull, insensitive. (3, 29–30)

~ Understanding ~

There is no intellectual understanding; either we understand, or we don't. (3, 21)

Understanding comes, not through the exertion of will, but only when the mind is still. (1, 86)

~ UNIVERSALITY ~

Whether we live east or west of a certain line, whether
we are brown, black, white, or yellow, we are all human
beings, suffering and hoping, fearful and believing; joy
and pain exist here as they exist there.   (2, 219)

Thought is not of the West or of the East, but man
divides it according to his conditioning. . . . The division of human beings is for economic and exploiting
purposes.   (2, 219–20)

~ THE UNKNOWN ~

The unknown is not the future, but the present. The
future is but the past pushing its way through the
uncertain present.   (1, 21)

The unknown is not to be caught in the net of the
known. Knowledge must be set aside for the unknown
to be; but how difficult that is!   (1, 20)

What is of the highest importance is to let the unknown come into being. (2, 285)

The unknowable doesn't invite you, and you cannot invite it. It comes and goes as the wind, and you cannot capture it and store it away for your benefit, for your use. (2, 258–59)

~ VEGETARIANISM ~

The eating of flesh and fish involves the taking of life, often with cruelty . . . [having] become a need through custom, [it] must eventually induce a callous indifference towards suffering as a whole, and deaden the tender compassion which always characterizes the spiritual man. (Weeraperuma, *Living and Dying*, 94)

Meditation means attention, care. . . . Don't kill animals, don't kill them to eat, it's so unnecessary. (*A Wholly Different Way*, 269)

Here [in the West] animals have no souls, so they can be killed with impunity; there [in India] animals have souls, so consider and let your hearts know love. (2, 236)

~ VIOLENCE ~

Violence must cease for love to be. The cessation of violence is not a matter of time. (3, 11)

Our present relationship [to one other] is based on need and use. Such a relationship is inherently violent, and that is why the very basis of our society is violence. (2, 82)

~ VIRTUE ~

Virtue is the tranquility of freedom from the craving to be, and this tranquility is of the heart, not of the mind. (1, 30)

A virtue that is cultivated ceases to be a virtue, for then it is merely another form of achievement, a record to be made. A cultivated virtue is not the abnegation of the self but a negative assertion of the self. (1, 13)

~ Visions ~

If you are a Christian, your visions follow a certain pattern; if you are a Hindu, a Buddhist, or a Muslim, they follow a different pattern. You see Christ or Krishna, according to your conditioning; your education, the culture in which you have been brought up, determines your visions. (3, 197)

~ Vulnerability ~

There must be vulnerability to meet life, and not the respectable wall of self-enclosing virtue. (1, 29–30)

That which is open and vulnerable is beautiful; the enclosed is dull and insensitive. (1, 183)

To be vulnerable is to live, and to withdraw is to die. (2, 108)

~ What *Is* ~

It is the experiencing of what *is* without naming it that brings about freedom from what *is*. (1, 54)

The recognition of what *is* does not lead to smug contentment and ease. (1, 125)

What you are is much more important than what you should be. (1, 139)

The what *is* is deathless. (1, 267)

What *is* is never complex in itself; it is always simple. (1, 241)

~ WILL ~

Will is desire, and it can tyrannically dominate all other desires; but what is thus conquered has to be conquered again and again.   (3, 353)

~ WISDOM ~

Self-knowledge is the beginning of wisdom; [when we are] without self-knowledge, learning leads to ignorance, strife, and sorrow.   (2, 3)

The love of what *is* is the beginning of wisdom.
(1, 182)

There is no path to wisdom.   (1, 103)

Wisdom is when knowledge ends.   (1, 254)

Thinking is an impediment to experiencing; and there is no wisdom without experiencing. Knowledge, idea, belief, stand in the way of wisdom. (1, 189)

~ WORDS ~

Words fill our libraries; and how incessantly we talk! We hardly dare to be without a book, to be unoccupied, to be alone. (1, 88–89)

Words are satisfying because their sounds reawaken forgotten sensations; and their satisfaction is greater when words are substituted for the actual, for what *is*. (1, 88)

We try to fill our inward emptiness with words, with sound, with noise, with activity; music and the chant are a happy escape from ourselves, from our pettiness and boredom. (1, 88)

~ Worry ~

If we did not worry, most of us would feel that we were not alive; to be struggling with a problem is for the majority of us an indication of existence. We cannot imagine life without a problem.   (1, 7)

For most people, a quiet mind is a rather fearsome thing; they are afraid to be quiet, for heaven knows what they may discover in themselves, and worry is a preventive.   (1, 7)

~ Worship ~

To worship another is to worship oneself; the image, the symbol, is a projection of oneself.   (2, 47)

Your image is your intoxicant, and it is carved out of your own memory; you are worshipping yourself through the image created by your own thought.
        (2, 48)

~ You Are the World ~

The individual is essentially the collective, and society is the creation of the individual. The individual and society are interrelated, are they not?   (2, 97)

The problem of the individual is also the world's problem, they are not two separate and distinct processes.   (2, 202)

You are the repository of all humanity. You are the world, and the world is you. And, if there is a radical transformation in the structure of an individual's psyche, it will affect the whole consciousness of man.
(Krishnamurti at Rajghat, 86)

BIBLIOGRAPHY

It is the editor's hope that this accessible, yet provocative, introduction to Krishnamurti's teachings will prompt the reader to consult the original sources listed here as well as those in the suggested further reading section.

Anderson, Allan W., and J. Krishnamurti. *A Wholly Different Way of Living: J. Krishnamurti in Dialogue with Professor Allan W. Anderson*. Brockwood Park, UK: Krishnamurti Foundation Trust, 1991.

Krishnamurti (Alcyone). *At the Feet of the Master and Towards Discipleship*. Rev. ed. Wheaton, IL: Quest, 2001.

———. *Commentaries on Living*, First Series. Wheaton, IL: Quest, 1967. Page references are to the 2006 reprint.

———. *Commentaries on Living*, Second Series. Wheaton, IL. Quest, 1967. Page references are to the 2002 reprint.

———. *Commentaries on Living*, Third Series. Wheaton, IL: Quest, 1967. Page references are to the 2007 reprint.

———. *The First and Last Freedom*. Wheaton, IL: Quest, 1968.

———. *Total Freedom: The Essential Krishnamurti*. San Francisco: HarperSanFrancisco, 1966.

———. *What Are You Doing with Your Life?* Vol. 1. Dale Bick Carlson and Kishore Khairnar, eds. Ojai, CA: Krishnamurti Foundation of America, 2001.

Krishnamurti Foundation India. *Krishnamurti at Rajghat*. Madras, India: Krishnamurti Foundation India, 1993.

Lutyens, Mary. *Krishnamurti: The Years of Awakening*. Boston: Shambhala, 1997.

Ravindra, Ravi. *Krishnamurti: Two Birds on One Tree*. Wheaton, IL: Quest, 1995.

Sloss, Radha Rajagopal. *Lives in the Shadow with J. Krishnamurti*. London: Bloomsbury, 1991.

Weeraperuma, Susunaga. *Living and Dying From Moment to Moment: An Investigation of J. Krishnamurti's Teaching*. Bombay: Motilal Banarsidass, 1978.

Suggested Further Reading

Dozens of books by and about Krishnamurti have been published, and what follows is not an exhaustive list but rather a sampling that the editor has read over a thirty-year period.

Brau, Evelyn. *Krishnamurti: 100 Years.* New York: Stewart, Tabori & Chang, 1995.

Jayakar, Pupul. *Krishnamurti: A Biography.* San Francisco: Harper & Row, 1986.

Kreimer, J. Carlos. *Krishnamurti for Beginners.* New York: Writers and Readers Publishing, 1997.

Krishnamurti, Jiddu. *The Awakening of Intelligence.* San Francisco: HarperSanFrancisco, 1973.

———. *Beyond Violence.* New York: Harper & Row, 1973.

———. *The Book of Life.* San Francisco: HarperSan-
Francisco, 1995.

———. *Can Humanity Change?* Boston: Shambhala,
2003.

———. *Facing a World in Crisis.* Boston: Shambhala,
2005.

———. *The Flame of Attention.* San Francisco: Harper
& Row, 1983.

———. *The Flight of the Eagle.* New York: Harper &
Row, 1972.

———. *Freedom from the Known.* New York: Harper &
Row, 1969.

———. *The Future of Humanity.* San Francisco: Harper
& Row, 1989.

———. *Inward Revolution.* Boston: Shambhala, 2006.

———. *Life Ahead: On Learning and the Search for
Meaning.* Novato, CA: New World Library, 1963.

———. *On Fear.* San Francisco: HarperSanFrancisco,
1995

———. *On God.* San Francisco: HarperSanFrancisco,
1992.

———. *On Living and Dying.* Sandpoint, ID: Morning
Light Press, 2005.

———. *On Love and Loneliness.* San Francisco: Harper-SanFrancisco, 1993.

———. *Questioning Krishnamurti.* San Francisco: Thorsons, 1996.

———. *Talks with American Students.* Boston: Shambhala, 1988.

———. *Think on These Things.* New York: Harper & Row, 1964.

———. *This Light in Oneself.* Boston: Shambhala, 1999.

———. *The Wholeness of Life.* San Francisco: Harper-SanFrancisco, 1979.

Krishnamurti, Jiddu, and David Bohm. *The Ending of Time.* San Francisco: HarperSanFrancisco, 1985.

———. *The Limits of Thought.* NY: Routledge, 1999.

Krohnen, Michael. *The Kitchen Chronicles 1001 Lunches with J. Krishnamurti.* Ojai, CA: Edwin House, 1997.

———. *Krishnamurti: The Years of Fulfillment.* New York: Avon, 1991.

Smith, Ingram. *The Transparent Mind: A Journey with Krishnamurti.* Ojai, CA: Edwin House, 1999.

Vernon, Roland. *Star in the East: Krishnamurti, The Invention of a Messiah.* Boulder, CO: Sentient, 2002.

About the Compiler

Robert Epstein is a licensed psychologist as well as a haiku poet and freelance writer. He has been studying Krishnamurti's teachings for thirty years. He is the co-editor, with Sherry Phillips, of *The Natural Man,* an anthology of quotations of Henry D. Thoreau, also published by Quest Books. Robert lives in the San Francisco Bay area.

Related Quest Titles

Commentaries on Living, J. Krishnamurti

The Inner Life of J. Krishnamurti, Aryel Sanat

Krishnamurti: Two Birds on One Tree, Ravi Ravindra